The Super Easy Baking Cookbook for Teens

1000 Days Sweet and Savory Recipes for the Home Baker for Breads, Cakes, Biscuits, Pies, and More
A Baking Book

Erma Catis

© Copyright 2021 Erma Catis - All Rights Reserved.

In no way is it legal to reproduce, duplicate, or transmit any part of this document by either electronic means or in printed format. Recording of this publication is strictly prohibited, and any storage of this material is not allowed unless with written permission from the publisher. All rights reserved.

The information provided herein is stated to be truthful and consistent, in that any liability, regarding inattention or otherwise, by any usage or abuse of any policies, processes, or directions contained within is the solitary and complete responsibility of the recipient reader. Under no circumstances will any legal liability or blame be held against the publisher for any reparation, damages, or monetary loss due to the information herein, either directly or indirectly.

Respective authors own all copyrights not held by the publisher.

Legal Notice:

This book is copyright protected. This is only for personal use. You cannot amend, distribute, sell, use, quote or paraphrase any part of the content within this book without the consent of the author or copyright owner. Legal action will be pursued if this is breached.

Disclaimer Notice:

Please note the information contained within this document is for educational and entertainment purposes only. Every attempt has been made to provide accurate, up-to-date and reliable, complete information. No warranties of any kind are expressed or implied. Readers acknowledge that the author is not engaging in the rendering of legal, financial, medical or professional advice.

By reading this document, the reader agrees that under no circumstances are we responsible for any losses, direct or indirect, which are incurred as a result of the use of information contained within this document, including, but not limited to, errors, omissions, or inaccuracies.

CONTENTS

INTRODUCTION 6

Part 1 7

The Basics Of Baking 7

Baking Techniques And Skills 11

Part 2 14

Breakfast Treats 14

    Baked Oatmeal 14

    Oatmeal Cookies 16

    Breakfast Hash 17

    Lemon Blueberry Muffins 18

    Ham And Cheese Egg Cups 20

    Morning Cinnabon 21

    Cherry Danish Muffins 23

    Breakfast Casserole Muffins 24

    Raspberry Breakfast Bars 25

    Oatmeal Protein Muffins 27

Cookies, Brownies, And Bars 28

    Sugar Cookies 28

    Lemon Shortbread Cookies 30

    Chewy Molasses Cookies 31

    Tahini Cookies 33

    Apple Squares 34

    Chocolate Chip Cookie Bars 36

    Vegan Brownies 37

    Chewy Peanut Butter Brownies 38

    Hermit Bar Cookies 39

    Pumpkin Pie Bars 41

Cakes, Cupcakes, And Cakes In A Jar 43

    Iced Fairy Cakes 43

    Raspberry Cupcakes With Orange Glaze 45

    Coconut Raspberry Cupcakes 46

    Lemon Pie Cake 47

    Apple Dump Cake 49

    Yoghurt Fruit Cake 50

    Blueberry Coffee Cake 51

    Chocolate Marble Pound Cake 53

    Chocolate Zucchini Cake 55

    Apple Pie Cake 56

Pies And Tarts 57

    Mini S'mores Pie 57

    Pumpkin Pie 58

    Mini Peach Raspberry Pies 60

    Pies On Stick 62

    Blackberry Pie 64

    Blueberry Pie 66

    Raspberry Pie 68

    Lemon Pie 70

    Southern Pecan Pie 71

    Baked Pudding Pie 72

Savory Breads And Shacks 73

    White Bread 73

    Vegan Banana Bread 74

    Mincemeat Banana Bread 75

    Gluten-Free Bread 76

    Coconut Cardamom Bread 77

    Sticky Toffee Bread 78

    Walnut Bread 80

    Zucchinis Cheddar Bread 81

Monkey Bread 82

Carrot Bread 84

Savory Pies, Tarts, And Pizza 85

Holiday Pizzas 85

Quick Pitta Pizzas 87

Rainbow Pizzas 88

Tuna Rocket Pizzas 89

Mozzarella, Ham Pesto Pizzas 90

Bacon Scone Pizza 91

Spinach Pizza 93

Spinach Blue Cheese Pizza 95

Cauliflower Cheese Pizza 96

Fiorentina Pizzas 97

Easy Dinners 98

Sausage Pasta Dinner 98

Baked Chicken Parmesan 99

Chicken Rice Casserole 100

Crispy Chicken Tenders 101

Creamy Pasta Bake 102

Roasted Salmon 103

Chicken Nuggets 104

Barbecued Chicken 105

Parsley Cod 106

Meat Loaf Muffins 107

CONCLUSION 108

INTRODUCTION

Baking fascinates us all! Getting to see our favorite muffins, cookies or cakes turning golden brown in the oven and hearing that ring once it's done cooking is the most exciting experience that every teenager must experience. This cookbook will lend you a much-needed insight regarding the whole baking process and how as a beginner, you can get started with it. There are several everyday recipes that you can easily try at home using some basic kitchen ingredients. There are breakfast meals, pies, cookies, cakes and dinner ideas that you can enjoy baking in your kitchen. So, let's get started!

PART 1

THE BASICS OF BAKING

Baking is a science that depends on basic knowledge of the baking process's principles. You'll be able to recreate recipes with greater ease after you grasp how each action influences the final product. To be a successful baker, you don't need a degree in chemistry or physics, but thorough awareness of the everyday science of the kitchen will give you a well-rounded understanding of baking. It's critical that you understand the scientific concepts underlying each activity that occurs when you combine flour, fat, and water to make a baked item.

Accuracy is of Essence

The same ingredients are used in almost all baked goods: flour, water, salt, fat, and leavening agents. The manner of assembling the ingredients can sometimes be the only variation between two products. The ratio of ingredients in a dish might also make a difference. Small modifications in the procedure and ratio can have a big impact on the baked good's quality. This is why it's critical to follow recipes exactly as written and accurately measure ingredients.

Measuring Ingredients

The importance of precise, exact ingredient measures cannot be overstated. It's critical to measure the ingredients precisely if you want to get the same result as the recipe author. The majority of recipes use either Imperial or metric measurements. Some recipe writers combine the two. If a recipe calls for both measurements, don't mix and match the ones you use. Make a decision and stick to it. Do not, for example, weigh the flour before measuring the rest of the ingredients in cups or ounces. This will result in measurement mistakes and have a detrimental impact on the final product.

Measuring With Perfection

Use plastic or stainless steel measuring cups to measure dry ingredients. Fluff the flour with a fork and lightly spoon it into the measuring cup. Allow the flour to mound rather than shaking the cup or packing it down. To level ingredients in the measuring cup, use a straight edge, such as a knife. Use a liquid measuring jug or cup with a pouring lip to measure liquid substances. Read the measurements at eye level by placing the cup on a flat surface. Use a measuring container that holds the exact amount of brown sugar specified in the recipe to measure it. Fill the dry measuring cup halfway with brown sugar and level it off with a straight edge. Coat the measuring cup with a little layer of cooking spray before measuring syrupy ingredients like honey, molasses, or corn syrup. This makes it easy for the component to escape.

The Importance Of Ingredient Temperature

You can use the best ingredients, measure them precisely, and mix them perfectly, but if the temperatures aren't kept under control, you risk failing. Temperature affects the characteristics of several components, particularly lipids. When producing batters and doughs, it's vital not only to temper eggs or yolks before adding them to custard but also to bring cold ingredients to room temperature. They emulsify easily when all of the ingredients are at the same temperature. As a consequence, you'll have a smooth, homogenous batter that bakes up beautifully. It's a good thumb rule to set these ingredients out on the counter unless a recipe specifically calls for them to be chilled.

Mixing Methods

The next step is to mix the components after they have been properly measured. To get the intended results, the ingredients must be blended in a certain order. The volume, look, and texture of the finished product are all influenced by the mixing technique you utilize.

Distributes the components evenly.

There are nine different mixing procedures, each with its own function. The materials are correctly blended by blending, folding, sieving, and stirring. Cutting the ingredients together also guarantees that the final dish bakes up flaky. Air is included in the batter by beating, creaming, kneading, and whipping. The baked good's ultimate texture is determined by the air pockets. Water and fats do not mix. Stirring, beating, creaming, mixing, and kneading, on the other hand, break up fats into particles, allowing them to mix with other liquids to form a homogeneous mixture. The batter should not be over-mixed. Allow batters to rest as necessary. Pay heed to the instructions in a recipe. The method used to combine the ingredients can make or break the final product.

Even Cooking

Heat will transform a thoroughly mixed batter or dough into a delectable baked treat. Make sure there's enough space between the pans in the oven for air to circulate freely. This helps to keep the oven temperature consistent and encourages even cooking. It's also crucial not to open and close the oven door during the baking process. When you open the oven's door, again and again, heat escapes, causing the temperature to drop.

Once a baked meal is removed from the oven, the baking process continues. The heated pan retains residual heat and will continue to bake as the product cools. This is why most cookie recipes warn that when you remove the cookies from the oven, they will appear undercooked. The cookies, however, will finish baking and become crisp as they cool.

Essential Baking Items

Before getting started with your whole baking experience, you must check whether you have the following supplies available in your kitchen. These utensils help in baking several different meals with complete ease and convenience:

- *Bake pans of different sizes*
- *Casserole dishes*
- *Cooling rack*
- *A dredger or shaker*
- *Icing smoother*
- *Food mixer*
- *Baking parchment sheet*
- *Food processor*
- *Marzipan spacers*
- *Cookie cutters*
- *Cake knives*
- *Stand mixer*
- *Hand whisk*
- *Mixing bowls*
- *Measuring cups*
- *Measuring spoons*
- *Calibrated jug for liquid measurements*
- *Muffin pans*
- *Muffin cup liners*
- *Piping bag*
- *Plastic wrap*

BAKING TECHNIQUES AND SKILLS

Whether you are baking bread, cookies or a delectable cake in your oven, there are certain techniques that help you bake like pros! Every beginner is susceptible to make mistakes, and that's ok if you mess up one or two times, but learning the following few tips, you will be able to get good results every time.

1. **Stick to The Recipe**

    Everything is covered in the recipe, from preheating the oven to whether or not to oil the pan. Yes, you should grease your pan frequently. However, there are situations when you should not. Using room temperature butter instead of cold butter has the same effect. Rather than trying to remember everything, including the multiple exceptions to each rule and the exceptions to the exceptions, just stick to the recipe. After all, that's why it's there in the first place.

2. **Measure Your Ingredients Properly**

    To accurately measure your ingredients, you must weigh them. This usually pertains to flour, which is the most important ingredient in baking and is notoriously difficult to accurately measure using volume measurements such as cups. Look for recipes that specify the exact measurements. Sure, you can convert the recipe, but odds are it will work better if it was written that way, to begin with. Use marked calibrated cups and spoons to measure properly.

3. **Use Fresh Ingredients**

    Using fresh ingredients always give your meal a better taste and texture. There are ingredients like eggs, milk and other dairy products that are used in baking, and they must be fresh. Ingredients like spices and dry powders are more shelf friendly, so you don't have to worry about their freshness.

4. Avoid Over-Mixing

Flour is used to make doughs and batters, and flour contains gluten, which gets more solid and stretchy as you stir, beat, knead, and so on. You could want it with pizza dough, but not so much with pie dough. The good news is that the recipe should tell you how much, how long, and how strongly you should mix your dough, so stick to it and learn how over-mixing can affect gluten.

5. Calibrate Your Oven

Make sure your oven is calibrated. The problem is that the temperature in your oven may not be what you set it to be. Your dish will not turn out properly if you set your oven to 350 degrees Fahrenheit, but it only heats up to 320 degrees Fahrenheit or even 380 degrees Fahrenheit. Although repairing the oven is a huge task, the option is to get a low-cost oven thermometer. Preheat it to 350 degrees Fahrenheit and check the temperature with a thermometer. If it's different, you can make the necessary adjustments.

6. Use a Light-Colored Pan

If at all possible, choose a light-colored pan. The dark-colored pans tend to absorb more heat than light-colored pans; as a result of this, the food, batter or cookies in such pan can get burnt from the bottom. The thing is that light-colored pan recipes have been written and tested. You can lower the temperature or lessen the cooking time if you only have dark-colored pans.

7. Use Unsalted Butter

Again, the recipe will almost probably state this, so make sure you follow it. However, if the recipe does not indicate, unsalted butter should be used. Salt not only influences the flavour of the dough, but it also changes the way the glutens in the flour grow, which can affect the consistency of the dough.

8. Scrape the Mixing Bowl

When mixing batter wit-h a stand mixer, you want to properly combine the ingredients, which can be difficult if major components of the recipe, such as butter, eggs, or sugar, are stuck to the sides of the bowl. Fortunately, scraping the mixing bowl every 30 seconds or so is a simple task.

9. Keep the Oven Closed

Keep the oven closed at all times. Looking inside to see how things are going is enticing, but it's not a good idea. The influx of air, or the vibration of the oven door, might cause a cake to tumble while baking. Some cooks suggest rotating cookie trays halfway through baking, but the benefit isn't worth the heat loss. Keep it shut.

PART 2

BREAKFAST TREATS

BAKED OATMEAL

Preparation Time: 10 minutes
Cooking Time: 30 minutes
Serve: 6

Ingredients:
- 2 large eggs
- 1/4 cup canola oil
- 1 cup packed brown sugar
- 1/2 cup applesauce
- 1 1/2 cups skim milk
- 2 teaspoons vanilla extract
- 1/2 teaspoons salt
- 1 tablespoon ground cinnamon
- 3 cups old fashioned rolled oats
- 2 teaspoons baking powder
- ¼ cup dried fruit
- ¼ cup nuts
- ¼ cup chocolate chips

Directions:
1. At 350 degrees F, preheat your oven.
2. Layer a muffin pan with muffin liners.
3. Beat eggs with sugar and oil in a large mixing bowl with a hand whisk until sugar is dissolved.
4. Stir in cinnamon, salt, vanilla, milk and apple sauce then continue mixing for 1 minute.
5. Add baking powder and oats then mix until all the ingredients make a thick batter.
6. Add ¼ cup of the oat batter to each muffin liner and add dried fruits and nuts on top.

7. Bake the muffins for 30 minutes in the preheated oven.

8. Allow the muffin pan to cool then transfer the muffins to a plate.

9. Serve.

Nutritional Value (Amount per Serving):
Calories 311; Fat 12.1g; Cholesterol 63mg; Carbohydrate 44.5g; Sugars 29g ; Protein 6.8g

OATMEAL COOKIES

Preparation Time: 15 minutes
Cooking Time: 12 minutes
Serve: 6

Ingredients:

- 2 cups gluten free rolled oats
- 3 large overripe bananas, mashed
- 1/2 cup peanut butter
- 1/4 cup chocolate chips

Directions:

1. At 350 degrees F, preheat your oven.
2. Layer a cookie sheet with parchment paper.
3. Mix mashed banana with peanut butter in a suitable mixing bowl.
4. Stir in rolled oats and chocolate chips, then stir well until evenly mixed.
5. Take a medium sized ice-cream scoop and take a scoop of the oat batter.
6. Transfer the batter onto your wet palm and roll it into a ball.
7. Make 7 more balls and place them on a greased baking sheet.
8. Press the balls into cookies and bake them for 12 minutes in the oven.
9. Serve.

Nutritional Value (Amount per Serving):

Calories 276; Fat 14.3g; Cholesterol 2mg; Carbohydrate 32.5g; Sugars 12.9g; Protein 8.9g

BREAKFAST HASH

Preparation Time: 10 minutes
Cooking Time: 55 minutes
Serve: 3

Ingredients:

Potatoes

- 3 medium russet potatoes, peeled and diced
- 1 large sweet potato, peeled and diced
- 1 tablespoon onion powder
- 1 tablespoon garlic powder
- 1 teaspoon dried thyme
- 2 teaspoons sea salt
- 1 teaspoon pepper
- 1/4 cup olive oil

Garlic and onion mixture

- 1 medium onion, diced
- 5 garlic cloves, minced
- 1 teaspoon olive oil
- sprinkle of salt and black pepper

Directions:

1. At 450 degrees F, preheat your oven.
2. Toss potatoes with ¼ cup olive oil and spices in a greased baking dish.
3. Bake the potatoes for 50 minutes in the oven, toss the potatoes after every 20 minutes.
4. Sauté garlic with onion, black pepper, salt and oil in a skillet for 5 minutes.
5. Toss in baked potatoes and mix well.
6. Serve warm.

Nutritional Value (Amount per Serving):

Calories 387; Fat 17.3g; Cholesterol 0mg; Carbohydrate 55.5g; Sugars 9.5g; Protein 6.3g

LEMON BLUEBERRY MUFFINS

Preparation Time: 15 minutes
Cooking Time: 20 minutes
Serve: 6

Ingredients:

- 1 ½ cups all-purpose flour
- 2 teaspoons baking powder
- 1/4 teaspoon salt
- 2/3 cup granulated sugar
- 1 tablespoon grated lemon zest
- 2 eggs
- 2/3 cup Greek yogurt
- 1/3 cup vegetable oil
- 1 teaspoon vanilla extract
- 2 tablespoons fresh lemon juice
- 1 1/3 cups blueberries
- 1 tablespoon flour

Directions:

1. At 400 degrees F, preheat your oven.

2. Place paper liner in a 12 cup muffin pan.

3. Mix cinnamon, melted butter, sugar and flour in a bowl for 1 minute to make a crumbly mixture.

4. For muffin batter, mix salt, baking powder and flour in a bowl.

5. Mix eggs with sugar and lemon zest in a medium bowl with a hand whisk until sugar is dissolved.

6. Stir in vanilla, lemon juice, oil and yogurt then mix for 1 minute.

7. Stir in dry flour mixture, whisk well until smooth.

8. Keep ½ cup blueberries aside and add the remaining to the flour batter.

9. Mix evenly then divide the batter in the muffin cups.

10. Drizzle an equal amount of the crumbly flour mixture on of the muffin batter.

11. Divide the reserved berries on top of the batter and bake for 5 minutes.

12. Reduce the oven's temperature to around 375 degrees F then continue baking for 15 minutes in the oven.

13. Allow the muffins to cool then serve.

Nutritional Value (Amount per Serving):

Calories 368; Fat 14.5g; Cholesterol 56mg; Carbohydrate 53.5g; Sugars 27.2g; Protein 7.6g

HAM AND CHEESE EGG CUPS

Preparation Time: 10 minutes
Cooking Time: 30 minutes
Serve: 6

Ingredients:

- 20 oz. refrigerated hash browns
- 1 1/2 cup grated cheddar cheese
- 1 cup ham, cubed
- 8 eggs
- 1 teaspoon salt
- 1/2 teaspoons black pepper
- 1/4 teaspoons garlic powder
- 2 tablespoons milk

Directions:

1. At 350 degrees F, preheat your oven.

2. Beat eggs with black pepper, salt, garlic powder, and milk in a suitable bowl.

3. Stir in ham, grated cheese and hash browns.

4. Grease a muffin pan with cooking oil and divide the egg mixture into it.

5. Bake the egg muffins for 30 minutes in the preheated oven.

6. Serve warm.

Nutritional Value (Amount per Serving):

Calories 267; Fat 18.2g; Cholesterol 258mg; Carbohydrate 7.7g; Sugars 1.8g; Protein 18.2g

MORNING CINNABON

Preparation Time: 10 minutes
Cooking Time: 15 minutes
Serve: 12

Ingredients:

- 1 cup milk
- 2 eggs
- ⅓ cup butter
- 4 cups bread flour
- ½ teaspoon salt
- ½ cup white sugar
- 1 package active dry yeast

Filling

- 1 cup brown sugar packed
- 3 tablespoons ground cinnamon
- ⅓ cup butter softened

Frosting

- 4 ounce cream cheese softened
- ¼ cup butter softened
- 1 ½ cups confectioners' sugar
- ½ teaspoon vanilla extract
- ⅛ teaspoon salt

Directions:

1. Mix 2 cups flour with yeast in a large mixing bowl.

2. Warm milk in a saucepan and stir in salt, sugar and butter, until the butter is melted.

3. Pour this milk mixture into the flour.

4. Stir in eggs and use an electric mixer on low speed for 30 seconds to get a dough.

5. Knead this prepared dough on a lightly floured surface for 5 minutes.

6. Place this dough in a greased bowl then cover with a plastic sheet.

7. Leave the dough for 15 minutes.

8. Mix cinnamon and brown sugar for filling in a bowl.
9. Roll the prepared dough in 18x21 inch rectangle.
10. Spread the butter for filling on top of the dough.
11. Drizzle the cinnamon-sugar mixture and on top.
12. Roll the rectangle by holding one long side to get an 18inches long log.
13. Cut this roll into 12 slices.
14. Place the cinnamon roll slices in a baking sheet, cover them with a kitchen towel.
15. Leave them for 45 minutes.
16. During this time, preheat your oven at 400 degrees F.
17. Uncover the rolls and bake them for 15 minutes.
18. Meanwhile, beat cream cheese with salt, vanilla, butter, and sugar in a bowl using an electric beater until the mixture gets fluffy.
19. Divide the frosting on top of the cinnamon rolls.
20. Serve.

Nutritional Value (Amount per Serving):
Calories 355; Fat 17.2g; Cholesterol 67mg; Carbohydrate 46.8g; Sugars 36.8g; Protein 5.9g

CHERRY DANISH MUFFINS

Preparation Time: 10 minutes
Cooking Time: 11 minutes
Serve: 8

Ingredients:
- 1 roll (8 count) of Buttermilk Biscuits
- 1/2 cup + 2 tablespoons sugar
- 4 oz. cream cheese, softened
- 1/4 cup tart cherry preserves

Directions:
1. At 350 degrees F, preheat your oven.
2. Grease 8-cup muffin tray with cooking spray.
3. Beat cream cheese with sugar in a bowl using a hand mixer for 3 minutes.
4. Spread 2 tablespoons remaining sugar in a plate.
5. Unroll the biscuits and coat their one side with sugar.
6. Press each biscuit in a muffin cup and add 2 teaspoons cream cheese mixture in each cup.
7. Add a teaspoons of cherry preserve on top of the cream cheese filling.
8. Bake the muffin cups for 11 minutes in the preheated oven.
9. Allow the Danish muffins to cool for 5 minutes.
10. Serve.

Nutritional Value (Amount per Serving):
Calories 204; Fat 9.5g; Cholesterol 16mg; Carbohydrate 28.6g; Sugars 16.3g; Protein 3.1g

BREAKFAST CASSEROLE MUFFINS

Preparation Time: 10 minutes
Cooking Time: 18 minutes
Serve: 8

Ingredients:

- 4 pieces whole wheat bread, torn
- 4 deli ham slices, chopped
- 1 cup cheddar cheese, shredded
- 8 large eggs
- 1 cup milk
- 2 teaspoons ground mustard
- 1/2 teaspoon black pepper
- Dried parsley, for garnish

Directions:

1. At 400 degrees F, preheat your oven.

2. Grease a muffin pan with cooking oil.

3. Divide an equal amount of bread pieces, ham and cheese in the muffin cups.

4. Beat eggs with black pepper, milk and mustard in a bowl.

5. Pour this mixture in the prepared muffin cups and drizzle dried parsley on top.

6. Bake these bread muffins for 18 minutes in the preheated oven.

7. Serve warm.

Nutritional Value (Amount per Serving):

Calories 205; Fat 11.7g; Cholesterol 213mg; Carbohydrate 8.2g; Sugars 2.7g; Protein 16.2g

RASPBERRY BREAKFAST BARS

Preparation Time: 10 minutes
Cooking Time: 25 minutes
Serve: 12

Ingredients:
- ½ cup coconut oil
- ¾ cup pure maple syrup
- 1 teaspoon pure vanilla extract
- ½ cup 2 tablespoons sliced almonds
- 1 ½ cups white whole wheat flour
- 1 ½ cups old fashioned oats
- ½ teaspoon ground cinnamon
- ½ teaspoon baking soda
- ¼ teaspoon kosher salt
- 1 cup seedless raspberry jam
- 1 cup raspberries, fresh

Directions:
1. At 350 degrees F, preheat your oven.
2. Layer a 9 inch rectangular baking pan with a foil sheet then grease with oil.
3. Set up a hand mixer and add coconut oil and maple syrup to this bowl.
4. Beat these ingredients together for 3 minutes on medium-high speed.
5. Add vanilla then beat for 30 seconds.
6. Mix salt, baking soda, cinnamon, oats, flour and ½ cup almonds in a separate bowl.
7. Add this dry mixture to the coconut oil mixture and mix on low speed for 1 minute.
8. Keep 1 ¼ cup of this mixture aside and spread the remaining in the prepared pan.
9. Melt the jam in a microwave safe bowl by heating for 15 seconds in the microwave on high heat.
10. Spread this jam over the crust in the pan.

11. Spread the remaining oat mixture on top and drizzle 2 tablespoons sliced almonds on top.

12. Bake for almost 25 minutes in the preheated oven.

13. Slice into squares and serve.

Nutritional Value (Amount per Serving):

Calories 367; Fat 12.6g; Cholesterol 0mg; Carbohydrate 59.2g; Sugars 27.4g; Protein 5.2g

OATMEAL PROTEIN MUFFINS

Preparation Time: 15 minutes
Cooking Time: 25 minutes
Serve: 12

Ingredients:
- 3 cups rolled oats
- 1 teaspoon baking powder
- 1 cup almond milk
- 2 eggs
- 1 scoop whey protein vanilla flavor
- 1/2 cup maple syrup
- Cooking spray
- 1 cup fresh fruit
- Maple syrup for serving

Directions:
1. At 350 degrees F, preheat your oven.
2. Grease a suitable 12-cup muffin tray with cooking spray.
3. Mix oats with protein powder, and baking powder in a large bowl.
4. Stir in maple syrup, eggs and milk then mix well with a fork.
5. Divide this oat mixture in the prepared muffin pan.
6. Bake the oatmeal muffins for 25 minutes in the preheated oven.
7. Allow the muffins to cool and serve.

Nutritional Value (Amount per Serving):
Calories 183; Fat 7g; Cholesterol 29mg; Carbohydrate 25.9g; Sugars 9.9g; Protein 5.7g

COOKIES, BROWNIES, AND BARS

SUGAR COOKIES

Preparation Time: 10 minutes
Cooking Time: 10 minutes
Serve: 12

Ingredients:
- 2¾ cups all-purpose flour
- 1 teaspoon baking soda
- 1 teaspoon cream of tartar
- ½ teaspoon sea salt
- 1 cup butter, softened
- ¾ cup powdered sugar
- 1 large egg
- 1 teaspoon vanilla extract
- 1 teaspoon almond extract
- 1 tablespoon lemon zest

Directions:
1. At 350 degrees F, preheat your oven.
2. Layer two baking sheets with parchment paper.
3. Mix cream of tartar, salt, baking soda and flour in a medium bowl.
4. Blend butter in a bowl of the stand mixer until fluffy.
5. Stir in sugar and beat for 2 minutes.
6. Scrape off the sides of the bowl then add egg, vanilla, almond extract and lemon zest.
7. Beat these ingredients together until mix well and stir in all the dry ingredients.
8. Mix well until it makes a rough dough.
9. Cover the dough bowl with a plastic wrap and refrigerate for 2 hours.
10. Roll out the dough into ¼ inch thick sheet and cut cookies out using a cookie cutter.

11. Place the cookies in the baking sheets and bake for 10 minutes.
12. Allow the cookies to cool then serve.

Nutritional Value (Amount per Serving):
Calories 277; Fat 16.1g; Cholesterol 56mg; Carbohydrate 29.7g; Sugars 7.5g; Protein 3.7g

LEMON SHORTBREAD COOKIES

Preparation Time: 10 minutes
Cooking Time: 14 minutes
Serve: 8

Ingredients:

- ½ cup butter, softened
- ⅓ cup cane sugar
- Zest of 1 medium lemon
- 1 tablespoon fresh lemon juice
- 1 tablespoon fresh thyme leaves, chopped
- 1¼ cups all-purpose flour
- ¼ teaspoon sea salt

Directions:

1. At 350 degrees F, preheat your oven.
2. Layer a baking sheet with parchment paper.
3. Blend butter in a bowl of an electric mixer for 2 minutes.
4. Stir in sugar and beat until fluffy.
5. Scrap off the sides then add lemon juice, zest, thyme, leaves, flour and salt.
6. Mix well until there is a sticky dough then knead it over a floured surface.
7. Cover and refrigerate the dough for 30 minutes.
8. Roll the dough into ¼ inch thick sheet and cut 2 inch round cookies using a cookie cutter.
9. Place the cookies in the baking sheet and bake for 14 minutes.
10. Allow the cookies to cool then serve.

Nutritional Value (Amount per Serving):

Calories 264; Fat 12g; Cholesterol 31mg; Carbohydrate 34.2g; Sugars 0.8g; Protein 4.7g

CHEWY MOLASSES COOKIES

Preparation Time: 10 minutes
Cooking Time: 10 minutes
Serve: 12

Ingredients:

- ½ cup soft coconut oil
- ⅓ cup packed brown sugar
- ⅓ cup granulated sugar
- ⅓ cup blackstrap molasses
- 1 teaspoon vanilla
- 2 cups all-purpose flour
- 2 teaspoons cinnamon
- 1 teaspoon baking soda
- 1 teaspoon ground ginger
- ½ teaspoon cardamom
- ½ teaspoon fine sea salt
- 1 tablespoon water

Directions:

1. At 350 degrees F, preheat your oven.

2. Layer a baking sheet with parchment paper.

3. Mix softened coconut oil, granulated sugar and brown sugar in the bowl of an electric mixture for 3 minutes.

4. Stir in vanilla and molasses then beat for 2 minutes.

5. Mix flour, salt, cardamom, ginger, baking soda, and cinnamon in another bowl.

6. Add this flour mixture to the mixer's bowl then add 1 tablespoon water.

7. Mix well to make a smooth dough.

8. Roll out the dough into ¼ inch thick sheet and cut 2 inch round cookies using a cookie cutter.

9. Place the cookies in the baking sheet and bake for 10 minutes.

10. Allow the cookies to cool and serve.

Nutritional Value (Amount per Serving):
Calories 240; Fat 9.3g; Cholesterol 0mg; Carbohydrate 36.3g; Sugars 16.3g; Protein 2.9g

TAHINI COOKIES

Preparation Time: 10 minutes
Cooking Time: 17 minutes
Serve: 8

Ingredients:
- ¾ cup tahini
- ½ cup maple syrup
- ½ teaspoon almond extract
- 2 cups almond flour
- ½ teaspoon cinnamon
- ¼ teaspoon ground cardamom
- ¼ teaspoon ground ginger
- ½ teaspoon baking powder
- ½ teaspoon sea salt
- ½ cup pomegranate arils

Directions:
1. At 350 degrees F, preheat your oven.
2. Layer a suitable baking sheet with parchment paper
3. Mix tahini with almond extract and maple syrup in a bowl with a hand mix.
4. Stir in salt, baking powder, ginger, cardamom, cinnamon and almond flour then mix well.
5. Drop 2 tablespoons of the cookie dough on the prepared baking sheet.
6. Add more cookie dough on the baking sheet in the same way, while keeping 1-2 inches distance between each.
7. Press the cookie dough with the bake of the spoon.
8. Drizzle pomegranate on top of the cookies and bake for 17 minutes in the preheated oven.
9. Allow the cookies to cool and serve.

Nutritional Value (Amount per Serving):
Calories 248; Fat 15.5g; Cholesterol 0mg ; Carbohydrate 24.9g; Sugars 16.9g; Protein 5.4g

APPLE SQUARES

Preparation Time: 10 minutes
Cooking Time: 30 minutes
Serve: 8

Ingredients:

- 1 cup sifted all-purpose flour
- 1 teaspoon baking powder
- ¼ teaspoon salt
- ¼ teaspoon ground cinnamon
- ¼ cup butter or margarine, melted
- ½ cup packed brown sugar
- ½ cup white sugar
- 1 egg
- 1 teaspoon vanilla extract
- ½ cup chopped apple
- ½ cup finely chopped walnuts
- 2 tablespoons white sugar
- 2 teaspoons ground cinnamon

Directions:

1. At 350 degrees F, preheat your oven.
2. Grease a 9x9 inches baking pan with cooking oil.
3. Mix flour with ¼ teaspoons cinnamon, salt and baking powder in a bowl.
4. Beat brown sugar with melted butter and ½ cup white sugar in a bowl using a hand mixer until sugar is dissolved.
5. Stir in vanilla and egg then beat for 1 minute.
6. Add the dry flour-cinnamon mixture then mix until smooth.
7. Fold in walnuts and apples then mix evenly.
8. Spread this apple batter in the prepared pan.
9. Mix remaining cinnamon and sugar in a bowl and drizzle over the batter.
10. Bake the batter for 30 minutes in the preheated oven.

11. Cut into squares and serve.

Nutritional Value (Amount per Serving):
Calories 248; Fat 10.9g; Cholesterol 36mg; Carbohydrate 35.6g ; Sugars 23.4g; Protein 4.2g

CHOCOLATE CHIP COOKIE BARS

Preparation Time: 10 minutes
Cooking Time: 40 minutes
Serve: 16

Ingredients:

- 1 cup butter, melted
- 1 cup dark brown sugar
- ½ cup white sugar
- 2 eggs
- 1 teaspoon vanilla extract
- 2 cups all-purpose flour
- 1 teaspoon baking soda
- 1 teaspoon salt
- ¼ teaspoon baking powder
- 2 cups dark chocolate chips

Directions:

1. At 350 degrees F, preheat your oven.
2. Grease a 9x13 inches baking dish.
3. Mix white and brown sugar and butter in a suitable bowl until sugar is dissolved.
4. Stir in eggs and vanilla then beat until creamy.
5. Stir in baking powder, salt, baking soda and flour then mix well.
6. Fold in chocolate chips then ix evenly.
7. Spread this chocolate chips batter in the prepared baking dish.
8. Bake this batter for 40 minutes in the preheated oven.
9. Allow the baked cookie batter to cool then cut into bars.
10. Serve.

Nutritional Value (Amount per Serving):

Calories 295; Fat 16.2g; Cholesterol 51mg; Carbohydrate 37.2g; Sugars 23.2g; Protein 3.4g

VEGAN BROWNIES

Preparation Time: 10 minutes
Cooking Time: 30 minutes
Serve: 12

Ingredients:
- 2 cups all-purpose flour
- 2 cups white sugar
- ¾ cup unsweetened cocoa powder
- 1 teaspoon baking powder
- 1 teaspoon salt
- 1 cup water
- 1 cup vegetable oil
- 1 teaspoon vanilla extract

Directions:
1. At 350 degrees F, preheat your oven.
2. Mix flour with salt, baking powder, sugar and cocoa powder in a large bowl.
3. Stir in vanilla, vegetable oil and water then mix until smooth.
4. Spread this batter in a 9x13 inches baking pan.
5. Bake the prepared batter for 30 minutes in the oven.
6. Slice into squares and serve.

Nutritional Value (Amount per Serving):
Calories 375; Fat 19.1g; Cholesterol 0mg; Carbohydrate 52.4g; Sugars 33.5g; Protein 3.2g

CHEWY PEANUT BUTTER BROWNIES

Preparation Time: 10 minutes
Cooking Time: 35 minutes
Serve: 12

Ingredients:
- ½ cup peanut butter
- ⅓ cup margarine, softened
- ⅔ cup white sugar
- ½ cup packed brown sugar
- 2 egg
- ½ teaspoon vanilla extract
- 1 cup all-purpose flour
- 1 teaspoon baking powder
- ¼ teaspoon salt

Directions:
1. At 350 degrees F, preheat your oven.
2. Grease a 9x9 inches baking pan with cooking oil.
3. Beat margarine with peanut butter in a bowl using a hand mixer.
4. Stir in eggs, vanilla, white sugar, and brown sugar then beat until fluffy.
5. Add salt, baking powder and flour then mix well until smooth.
6. Spread this batter in the prepared pan and bake for 35 minutes in the preheated oven.
7. Allow baked batter to cool then cut into 16 squares.
8. Serve.

Nutritional Value (Amount per Serving):
Calories 222; Fat 11.3g; Cholesterol 27mg; Carbohydrate 27.4g; Sugars 18.1g; Protein 4.8g

HERMIT BAR COOKIES

Preparation Time: 15 minutes
Cooking Time: 15 minutes
Serve: 12

Ingredients:
- ½ cup shortening
- 1 cup white sugar
- ½ cup molasses
- 1 teaspoon baking soda
- ½ cup warm coffee
- 1 egg
- 3 cups all-purpose flour
- ½ teaspoon salt
- 1 teaspoon ground cinnamon
- 1 teaspoon ground cloves
- 1 cup raisins

Directions:
1. At 350 degrees F, preheat your oven.
2. Grease a cookie sheet with cooking oil.
3. Beat shortening with sugar in a suitable bowl for 2 minutes with a hand mixer.
4. Stir in egg and molasses then mix until for 1 minute.
5. Mix warm coffee with baking soda in a bowl then pour into the egg mixture.
6. Add cloves, cinnamon, salt and flour then mix until the batter is smooth.
7. Fold in raisins and mix evenly.
8. Divide the dough into 4 equal portions.
9. Shape each portion into a long and press each into ¼ inch thick sheet.
10. Bake the dough for 15 minutes in the oven then cut each into bars.
11. Serve.

Nutritional Value (Amount per Serving):
Calories 334; Fat 9.3g; Cholesterol 14mg; Carbohydrate 60.6g; Sugars 31.5g; Protein 4.1g

PUMPKIN PIE BARS

Preparation Time: 10 minutes
Cooking Time: 60 minutes
Serve: 16

Ingredients:
- 4 large eggs
- 1 ½ cups white sugar
- 2 teaspoons ground cinnamon
- 1 teaspoon salt
- 1 teaspoon ground ginger
- ½ teaspoon ground cloves
- 1 (29 ounce) can pumpkin puree
- 2 (12 ounce) cans evaporated milk
- 1 (15 ¼ ounce) package yellow cake mix
- ½ cup butter, melted
- 1 (8 ounce) container whipped topping

Directions:
1. At 350 degrees F, preheat your oven.
2. Beat eggs in a suitable bowl with a hand mixer for 1 minute.
3. Mix cloves, ginger, salt, cinnamon and sugar in a bowl.
4. Add this mixture and pumpkin to the eggs then mix until sugar is dissolved.
5. Stir in evaporated milk and yellow cake mix then mix until smooth and lump-free.
6. Spread this batter in a greased 9x13 inch baking dish.
7. Bake it for 1 hour in the preheated oven.
8. Allow this cake to cool then cut into bars.
9. Garnish with whipped topping.
10. Serve.

Nutritional Value (Amount per Serving):

Calories 362; Fat 16.5g; Cholesterol 85mg; Carbohydrate 48.5g; Sugars 37.5g; Protein 6.3g

CAKES, CUPCAKES, AND CAKES IN A JAR

ICED FAIRY CAKES

Preparation Time: 15 minutes
Cooking Time: 20 minutes
Serve: 8

Ingredients:
- 3 ½ oz. caster sugar
- 3 ½ oz. very soft butter
- 3 ½ oz. self-rising flour
- 2 eggs
- 1 teaspoon vanilla extract

For the icing

- 7 oz. very soft butter
- 7 oz. icing sugar
- 2 drops green food coloring
- 1 tablespoon sprinkles

Directions:
1. At 350 degrees F, preheat your oven.
2. Layer a 12 cup muffin pan with cupcake liners.
3. Beat sugar with butter in a bowl with a hand mixer for 1 minute.
4. Stir in flour, eggs, and vanilla then mix until smooth.
5. Divide this batter into the muffin cups and bake for 20 minutes.
6. Meanwhile, beat butter with icing sugar in a bowl until creamy.
7. Stir in food coloring, mix well and transfer it to a piping bag with an icing nozzle.
8. Allow the cupcakes to cool and pipe the frosting on top of them.
9. Garnish with sprinkles.
10. Serve.

Nutritional Values:
Calories 216; Fat 11.5g; Cholesterol 68mg; Carbohydrate 26.2g; Sugars 16.6g; Protein 2.8g

RASPBERRY CUPCAKES WITH ORANGE GLAZE

Preparation Time: 15 minutes
Cooking Time: 25 minutes
Serve: 12

Ingredients:
- 7 oz. self-rising flour
- 2 teaspoons baking powder
- 7 oz. unsalted butter, softened
- 4 eggs
- 7 oz. caster sugar
- 3 tablespoons milk
- 1 2/3 oz. ground almond
- Zest of 1 medium orange
- 5 oz. punnet raspberry, crushed

Sugar Glaze

- juice of 1 medium orange
- 4 tablespoons caster sugar

Directions:
1. Place the muffin liners in a 12 cup muffin tray.
2. Beat eggs with sugar, milk and butter in a bowl with a hand mixer for 3 minutes.
3. Stir in ground almond, and orange zest then mix until smooth.
4. Fold in raspberries and divide this batter in the muffin cups.
5. Bake these muffins for 25 minutes in the preheated oven.
6. Meanwhile, mix orange juice and sugar in a bowl.
7. Brush this glaze over the muffins and serve.

Nutritional Values:
Calories 291; Fat 17.3g; Cholesterol 91mg; Carbohydrate 31g; Sugars 17.2g; Protein 4.7g

COCONUT RASPBERRY CUPCAKES

Preparation Time: 15 minutes
Cooking Time: 20 minutes
Serve: 12

Ingredients:

- 4 oz. self-rising flour
- 4 oz. caster sugar
- 1 2/3 oz. desiccated coconut
- 4 oz. butter, softened
- ½ teaspoons vanilla extract
- 2 large eggs
- 4 tablespoons milk
- 4 oz. raspberry, fresh or frozen

For the frosting

- 10 oz. icing sugar
- 2/3 oz. butter, softened
- 4 tablespoons raspberry coulis
- Shredded coconut, to decorate

Directions:

1. At 400 degrees F, preheat your oven.
2. Layer a 12 cup muffin pan with cupcake liners.
3. Mix all the batter ingredients in a bowl until smooth.
4. Divide this batter in the muffin cups and bake for 20 minutes in the oven.
5. Serve.

Nutritional Values:

Calories 314; Fat 13.3g; Cholesterol 57mg; Carbohydrate 47.4g; Sugars 35.2g; Protein 3.1g

LEMON PIE CAKE

Preparation Time: 15 minutes
Cooking Time: 45 minutes
Serve: 12

Ingredients:

- 1 lemon cake mix
- 1 (22 ounces) can lemon pie filling
- 1/2 cup buttermilk
- 4 large eggs

Fluffy Frosting

- 1/2 cup water
- 1 1/2 cups granulated sugar
- 2 tablespoons white corn syrup
- 3 large egg whites
- 1/2 teaspoon cream of tartar
- 1 1/2 teaspoons vanilla extract

Directions:

1. Grease 2-8 inches round cake pans then dust then with flour.
2. At 350 degrees F, preheat your oven.
3. Keep 1 cup of pie filling in a bowl in the refrigerator.
4. Mix remaining pie filling with eggs and buttermilk in a bowl.
5. Stir in cake mix and beat for 2 minutes with an electric mixer.
6. Divide this batter in the prepared pans and bake for 45 minutes in the preheated oven.
7. Allow the baked cakes to cool on a wire rack
8. Place one cake on a serving platter.
9. Spread the reserved pie filling on top and place the other cake on top.
10. Beat egg whites and rest of the frosting ingredients in a bowl with a beater until fluffy.
11. Spread the frosting over the cakes and serve.

Nutritional Values:
Calories 333; Fat 6.6g; Cholesterol 64mg ; Carbohydrate 64.7g; Sugars 52.5g; Protein 5.3g

APPLE DUMP CAKE

Preparation Time: 15 minutes
Cooking Time: 45 minutes
Serve: 14

Ingredients:
- 3/4 cup melted unsalted butter
- 5 medium apples, peeled, cored, and sliced
- 1 cup nuts of choice, lightly toasted
- 4 teaspoons ground cinnamon
- 1 teaspoon ground nutmeg
- 1/2 cup sugar
- 1 1/4 cups apple cider
- 1 (18-ounce) box yellow cake mix

Directions:
1. At 375 degrees F, preheat your oven.
2. Grease a 9x13 inches baking pan with some melted butter.
3. Toss apples with nuts and 2 teaspoons cinnamon, sugar and nutmeg in this pan.
4. Add apple cider, cakes mix and 2 teaspoons cinnamon on top of the apples.
5. Pour the melted butter on top and bake for 45 minutes in the preheated oven.
6. Serve.

Nutritional Values:
Calories 363; Fat 17.3g; Cholesterol 26mg; Carbohydrate 52g; Sugars 34.6g; Protein 4.2g

YOGHURT FRUIT CAKE

Preparation Time: 15 minutes
Cooking Time: 42 minutes
Serve: 12

Ingredients:

- 5 1/2 oz. raw sugar
- 2 Zest of 2 lemons
- 2 eggs
- 11 oz. yoghurt plain
- 3 1/2 oz. a light oil
- 10 1/2 oz. Self-Rising Flour
- 2 scoop Dried Fruit
- 1 scoop walnuts

Directions:

1. At 360 degrees F, preheat your oven.
2. Mix sugar, zest, eggs and yogurt in a bowl with a neater for 1 minute on medium speed.
3. Stir in oil, and flour then mix until smooth.
4. Fold in walnuts and dried fruit then mix evenly.
5. Grease a Bundt pan with cooking oil.
6. Add the prepared batter into the prepared pan.
7. Bake the batter for 42 minutes in the oven.
8. Allow the cake to cool then serve.

Nutritional Values:

Calories 258; Fat 9.8g; Cholesterol 27mg ; Carbohydrate 38.2g; Sugars 14.2g; Protein 5.8g

BLUEBERRY COFFEE CAKE

Preparation Time: 10 minutes
Cooking Time: 45 minutes
Serve: 12

Ingredients:

Streusel Topping

- 6 tablespoons packed light brown sugar
- 1/2 cup all-purpose flour
- 1 teaspoon ground cinnamon
- 1/4 teaspoon salt
- 4 tablespoons unsalted butter, diced

Cake

- 2 cups all-purpose flour
- 2 teaspoons baking powder
- 1/2 teaspoon salt
- 1/2 cup unsalted butter, softened
- 1 ½ teaspoons vanilla extract
- 3/4 cup granulated sugar
- 2 large eggs
- 1 teaspoon lemon zest
- 1/2 cup milk
- 2 cups fresh blueberries

Directions:

1. Mix streusel ingredients in a bowl and keep the mixture side.

2. At 375 degrees F, preheat your oven.

3. Grease a 9 inches baking pan with butter.

4. Mix flour, 2 tsp baking powder and salt in a medium bowl.

5. Beat butter with sugar in a suitable bowl with an electric mixture for 2 minutes.

6. Stir in eggs then beat for 3 minutes.

7. Stir in lemon zest, vanilla and flour mixture then mix well until smooth.

8. Fold in berries and mix evenly.

9. Spread this cake batter in the prepared pan then drizzle the streusel mixture on top.

10. Bake this cake for 45 minutes in the preheated oven.

11. Allow the cake to cool then serve.

Nutritional Values:

Calories 226; Fat 5.2g; Cholesterol 42mg ; Carbohydrate 41.4g; Sugars 19.9g; Protein 4.3g

CHOCOLATE MARBLE POUND CAKE

Preparation Time: 15 minutes
Cooking Time: 60 minutes
Serve: 8

Ingredients:
- 1/2 cup unsalted butter
- 1 cup granulated sugar
- 3 large eggs
- 1 teaspoon vanilla
- 1 3/4 cup all-purpose flour
- 2 teaspoons baking soda
- 1/2 teaspoons salt
- 1/4 cup cocoa powder
- 1/2 cup boiling water
- 2/3 cup buttermilk

Directions:
1. At 350 degrees F, preheat your oven.
2. Grease a loaf pan with butter.
3. Beat melted butter with sugar in a bowl with an electric mixer until fluffy.
4. Stir in vanilla and eggs then beat for 3 minutes.
5. Add soda, flour and salt then mix well until smooth.
6. Mix cocoa powder with boiling water in a bowl.
7. Add half of the prepared batter into the cocoa mixture then mix evenly until smooth.
8. Pour 1/3 of the white batter into the prepared pan.
9. Now add 1/3 of the brown batter followed by 1/3 white and brown batter.
10. Repeat this step and make swirls in the batter with a toothpick.
11. Bake the cake for 60 minutes in the preheated oven.
12. Allow the baked cake to cool then slice and serve.

Nutritional Values:
Calories 337; Fat 14.2g; Cholesterol 101mg; Carbohydrate 48.5g; Sugars 26.3g; Protein 6.5g

CHOCOLATE ZUCCHINI CAKE

Preparation Time: 15 minutes
Cooking Time: 60 minutes
Serve: 24

Ingredients:

- 2 cups all-purpose flour
- 2 cups white sugar
- ¾ cup unsweetened cocoa powder
- 2 teaspoons baking soda
- 1 teaspoon baking powder
- ½ teaspoon salt
- 1 teaspoon ground cinnamon
- 4 eggs
- 1 ½ cups vegetable oil
- 3 cups grated zucchini
- ¾ cup chopped walnuts

Directions:

1. At 350 degrees F, preheat your oven.
2. Layer a 9x13 inches baking pan with parchment paper and grease it with cooking oil.
3. Beat eggs with oil in a mixing bowl with hand whisk.
4. Add all the dry ingredients then mix well until smooth.
5. Fold in walnuts and zucchini then spread this batter in the pan.
6. Bake the cake for 60 minutes in the preheated oven.
7. Allow the baked cake to cool then slice and serve.

Nutritional Values:

Calories 260; Fat 14.5g; Cholesterol 27mg; Carbohydrate 45.4g; Sugars 31g; Protein 2.3g

APPLE PIE CAKE

Preparation Time: 5 minutes
Cooking Time: 75 minutes
Serve: 14

Ingredients:

- 1 (16-ounce) can whole cranberry sauce
- 1 (21-ounce) can apple pie filling
- 1 box yellow cake mix
- 4 ounces butter, softened
- 1/2 cup walnuts, or pecans, chopped

Directions:

1. At 325 degrees F, preheat your oven.
2. Grease a 13x9 inches baking pan with cooking spray.
3. Spread the cranberry sauce in the greased baking pan.
4. Add the apple pie filling on top.
5. Mix cake mix with butter in a bowl.
6. Spread this crumbly mixture over the filling and drizzle walnuts and pecans on top.
7. Bake the cake for 75 minutes in the preheated oven.
8. Serve.

Nutritional Values:

Calories 344; Fat 13.6g; Cholesterol 18mg; Carbohydrate 53g; Sugars 32.4g; Protein 2.8g

PIES AND TARTS

MINI S'MORES PIE

Preparation Time: 15 minutes
Cooking Time: 15 minutes
Serve: 6

Ingredients:
- 1 pie crust
- 2 graham crackers
- 6 marshmallows
- 1 chocolate bar

Directions:
1. At 375 degrees, preheat your oven.
2. Grease a muffin pan with cooking spray.
3. Unroll the premade pie crust and cut out 3 inches rounds out of this crust.
4. Place one round in each muffin cup and press it.
5. Crush the graham crackers and divide the crumbs in the muffin cups.
6. Add two rectangles and a marshmallow on top of the chocolate.
7. Bake the pies for 15 minutes in the preheat oven.
8. Allow the pies to cool then serve.

Nutritional Values:
Calories 271; Fat 12.6g; Cholesterol 2mg; Carbohydrate 37.6g; Sugars 22.7g; Protein 2.6g

PUMPKIN PIE

Preparation Time: 10 minutes
Cooking Time: 50 minutes
Serve: 12

Ingredients:

crust

- 8 tablespoons unsalted butter, melted
- 1 tablespoon vegetable oil
- 1 tablespoon granulated sugar
- 1/4 teaspoon fine salt
- 1 1/3 cups all-purpose flour

For the pie

- 1 (15-ounce) can pumpkin purée
- 1 (14-ounce) can sweetened condensed milk
- 2 large eggs
- 1 teaspoon ground cinnamon
- 1/2 teaspoon ground nutmeg
- 1/2 teaspoon fine salt
- 1/8 teaspoon ground clove

Directions:

1. Mix butter, sugar, oil and salt in a medium bowl.
2. Stir in flour, mix well to make a soft dough then knead the dough for 5 minutes.
3. Spread the dough into a 9 inches round pie plate.
4. Cover this crust with a plastic sheet and refrigerate for 30 minutes.
5. At 350 degrees F, preheat your oven.
6. Mix all the pie filling ingredients in a bowl with a hand whisk for 5 minutes.
7. Spread this filling in the refrigerated crust.
8. Bake this pie for 50 minutes in the preheated oven.
9. Allow the pie to cool then serve.

Nutritional Values:
Calories 255; Fat 12.7g; Cholesterol 63mg; Carbohydrate 30.7g; Sugars 19.5g; Protein 5.3g

MINI PEACH RASPBERRY PIES

Preparation Time: 10 minutes
Cooking Time: 35 minutes
Serve: 6

Ingredients:

- 4 prepared pie crust circles
- 12 oz fresh raspberries
- 2 lbs. fresh peaches, diced
- 1/4 cups flour
- 1/2 cups brown sugar
- 1/4 teaspoons salt

Topping

- 1 egg
- 1 tablespoon milk

Directions:

1. Cut about equal sized 24 circles out of the pie crust using a cookie cutter and place the circle in the muffin cup of a tray.
2. Cut small strips to make patterns on top of the mini pies using the leftover dough.
3. Place this muffin pan in the refrigerator until the filling is ready.
4. Mix peaches and raspberries with sugar, salt and flour in a bowl.
5. Divide the fruit filling in the refrigerated crusts.
6. Make lattice (crisscross) patterns on top of the pie filling using the crust strips.
7. At 400 degrees F, preheat your oven.
8. Beat egg with milk in a mini bowl and brush this mixture over the pies.
9. Bake these mini pies for 35 minutes in the preheated oven.
10. Serve.

Nutritional Values:

Calories 233; Fat 8.5g; Cholesterol 41mg; Carbohydrate 36.7g; Sugars 23g; Protein 3.5g

PIES ON STICK

Preparation Time: 10 minutes
Cooking Time: 15 minutes
Serve: 8

Ingredients:

- 4 unbaked 9-inch pie shells
- 1 egg white
- decorative sugar

Pumpkin pie filling

- 3/4 cup brown sugar
- 1/2 teaspoon kosher salt
- 1 teaspoon vanilla extract
- 2-1/2 teaspoons five-spice powder
- 2 large eggs
- 1 (15 ounce) can plain pumpkin
- 1 (12 ounce) can sweetened condensed milk

Directions:

1. At 375 degrees F, preheat your oven.
2. Mix five spice powder, salt and sugar in a small bowl.
3. Beat eggs with vanilla in another bowl.
4. Stir in sugar mixture, condensed milk and pumpkin.
5. Mix well and keep this mixture aside.
6. Spread the pie crusted on a floured surface.
7. Use a cookie cutter to cut 3-4 inches rounds out of each.
8. Place half of the crust rounds on a baking sheet lined with parchment paper.
9. Divide equal amount of filling at the center of each around.
10. Place the tip of a lollipop stick at the base of each round.
11. Place the other crust rounds on top of each filling pile and press the edges to seal.

12. Brush these pies with egg wash and drizzle sugar on top.

13. Bake the pie pops for 15 minutes in the preheated oven.

14. Serve.

Nutritional Values:
Calories 300; Fat 8.3g; Cholesterol 63mg; Carbohydrate 48.5g; Sugars 41.5g; Protein 7.5g

BLACKBERRY PIE

Preparation Time: 10 minutes
Cooking Time: 60 minutes
Serve: 6

Ingredients:
- 6 cups fresh blackberries rinsed
- 2 teaspoons lemon juice
- 1 cup granulated sugar
- ½ cup all-purpose flour
- 1 egg beaten
- 1 tablespoon cold butter, diced
- 2- 9" pie crusts

Egg wash

- 1 large egg beaten
- 1 tablespoon milk
- 1 pinch of salt

Topping

- 2 teaspoons turbinado sugar

Directions:
1. At 425 degrees F, preheat your oven.
2. Spread one pie crust in a 9 inches pie plate and fold the edges to make a rim.
3. Brush the crust with beaten egg and keep it aside.
4. Mix blackberries with flour and sugar in a bowl.
5. Spread this mixture in the crust and drizzle lemon juice on top.
6. Dot the cold butter pieces on top.
7. Roll out the other remaining pie crust and cut 8 strips for the pie topping.
8. Arrange the strips in a criss cross pattern to make a lattice on top.
9. Beat egg with milk and salt in a bowl and brush over the pie.

10. Drizzle sugar on top and bake for 15 minutes.

11. Now reduce the oven's temperature to 375 degrees F and bake for 45 minutes.

12. Allow the pie to cool then serve.

Nutritional Values:

Calories 164; Fat 13.1g; Cholesterol 0mg; Carbohydrate 12.2g; Sugars 4.9g; Protein 3g

BLUEBERRY PIE

Preparation Time: 10 minutes
Cooking Time: 60 minutes
Serve: 12

Ingredients:

- 5 1/2 cups fresh blueberries rinsed
- 1 tablespoon lemon juice
- 1 cup granulated sugar
- 1/3 cup tapioca flour
- 1/2 teaspoons cinnamon
- 1 egg beaten
- 1 tablespoon cold butter
- 2-9" pie crusts

Egg wash

- 1 large egg
- 1 tablespoon milk
- 1 pinch salt

Topping

- 2 teaspoons turbinado sugar

Directions:

1. At 425 degrees F, preheat your oven.
2. Spread one pie crust in a 9 inches pie plate and fold the edges to make a rim.
3. Brush the crust with beaten egg and keep it aside.
4. Mix blueberries with cinnamon, flour and sugar in a bowl.
5. Spread this mixture in the crust and drizzle lemon juice on top.
6. Dot the cold butter pieces on top.
7. Roll out the other remaining pie crust and cut 8 strips for the pie topping.
8. Arrange the strips in a criss cross pattern to make a lattice on top.
9. Beat egg with milk and salt in a bowl and brush over the pie.

10. Drizzle sugar on top and bake for 15 minutes.

11. Now reduce the oven's temperature to 375 degrees F and bake for 45 minutes.

12. Allow the pie to cool then serve.

Nutritional Values:

Calories 115; Fat 2.4g; Cholesterol 18mg; Carbohydrate 23.4g; Sugars 18.8g; Protein 1.2g

RASPBERRY PIE

Preparation Time: 10 minutes
Cooking Time: 60 minutes
Serve: 8

Ingredients:

- 6 cups fresh raspberries rinsed
- 2 teaspoons lemon juice
- 1 cup granulated sugar
- 4 tablespoons cornstarch
- 1 egg
- 1 tablespoon cold butter, diced
- 1 tablespoon milk
- 1 pinch salt
- 2 teaspoons turbinado sugar
- 2 (9 inches) pie crusts

Directions:

1. At 425 degrees F, preheat your oven.
2. Spread one pie crust in a 9 inches pie plate and fold the edges to make a rim.
3. Brush the crust with beaten egg and keep it aside.
4. Mix raspberries with cornstarch, and sugar in a bowl.
5. Spread this mixture in the crust and drizzle lemon juice on top.
6. Dot the cold butter pieces on top.
7. Roll out the other remaining pie crust and cut 8 strips for the pie topping.
8. Arrange the strips in a criss cross pattern to make a lattice on top.
9. Beat egg with milk and salt in a bowl and brush over the pie.
10. Drizzle sugar on top and bake for 15 minutes.
11. Now reduce the oven's temperature to 375 degrees F and bake for 45 minutes.
12. Allow the pie to cool then serve.

Nutritional Values:
Calories 242; Fat 3.5g; Cholesterol 33mg; Carbohydrate 54g; Sugars 39.9g; Protein 2.5g

LEMON PIE

Preparation Time: 10 minutes
Cooking Time: 45 minutes
Serve: 8

Ingredients:
- 2 medium lemons, peeled, sliced, seeds removed
- 2 cups sugar
- 1/2 cup butter, softened
- 4 large eggs
- 1 teaspoon vanilla extract
- 1 (9 -inches) pie crust

Directions:
1. At 350 degrees F, preheat your oven.
2. Spread the pie crust in a greased 9 inches pie plate and fold the edges to make the rim.
3. Blend with vanilla, butter and sugar in a blender .
4. Spread this mixture in the pie crust and bake for 45 minutes in the oven.
5. Allow the pie to cool then serve.

Nutritional Values:
Calories 207; Fat 14.6g; Cholesterol 0mg; Carbohydrate 17.7g; Sugars 6.1g; Protein 7g

SOUTHERN PECAN PIE

Preparation Time: 10 minutes
Cooking Time: 45 minutes
Serve: 8

Ingredients:
- 3 large eggs
- 1 1/2 cups granulated sugar
- 1/2 cup all-purpose flour
- 6 tablespoons unsalted butter melted
- 1 teaspoon vanilla extract
- 1/2 teaspoons salt
- 1/2 teaspoons lemon juice
- 1 cup light corn syrup
- 3 cups chopped pecans
- 1 (9 ") single pie crust

Directions:
1. At 350 degrees F, preheat your oven.
2. Grease a 10 inches cast iron skillet and spread the pie crust in it.
3. Beat eggs in a beater until fluffy.
4. Stir in corn syrup, lemon juice, salt, vanilla, melted butter, sugar and flour then mix well.
5. Fold in pecans and spread this mixture in the pie crust shell then bake for 45 minutes in the oven.
6. Allow the pie to cool then serve.

Nutritional Values:
Calories 255; Fat 13.8g; Cholesterol 0mg; Carbohydrate 27.2g; Sugars 5.2g; Protein 3.2g

BAKED PUDDING PIE

Preparation Time: 10 minutes
Cooking Time: 15 minutes
Serve: 8

Ingredients:

- 15 oz. pumpkin can
- 7 oz. Vanilla instant pudding mix
- 8 oz. cool whip
- 1 teaspoon pumpkin pie spice
- 1 graham cracker pie crust

Directions:

1. At 350 degrees F, preheat your oven.
2. Mix pumpkin with vanilla pudding mix, cool whip and pie spice in a bowl.
3. Spread the graham cracker crust in the greased pie plate.
4. Spread the filling in the crust and bake for 15 minutes in the oven.
5. Serve.

Nutritional Values:

Calories 312; Fat 1.9g; Cholesterol 0mg; Carbohydrate 28.3g; Sugars 15.7g; Protein 4.9g

SAVORY BREADS AND SHACKS

WHITE BREAD

Preparation Time: 15 minutes
Cooking Time: 35 minutes
Serve: 6

Ingredients:
- 1 lb. strong white bread flour
- 1 sachet dried yeast
- 1 teaspoon salt
- 2 tablespoons olive oil
- 1 tablespoon honey

Directions:
1. Mix flour, salt, and yeast with hot water, honey and oil in a mixing bowl.
2. Knead the prepared dough for 5 minutes on a floured surface.
3. Place this dough in a greased bowl, cover with a plastic sheet and leave for 1 hour.
4. Punch dough the dough and place it in a greased loaf pan.
5. At 425 degrees F, preheat your oven.
6. Make slashes on top of the dough and bake for 35 minutes.
7. Serve.

Nutritional Value (Amount per Serving):
Calories 330; Fat 5.8g; Cholesterol 0mg; Carbohydrate 60.2g; Sugars 4g; Protein 10.1g

VEGAN BANANA BREAD

Preparation Time: 10 minutes
Cooking Time: 40 minutes
Serve: 6

Ingredients:

- 3 large black bananas
- 1/3 cups vegetable oil
- 3 1/2 oz. brown sugar
- 8 oz. plain flour
- 3 heaped teaspoons baking powder
- 3 teaspoons cinnamon powder
- 1 2/3 oz. dried fruit

Directions:

1. At 425 degrees F, preheat your oven.
2. Mash 3 bananas in a suitable bowl then stir in sugar and oil.
3. Mix well then add flour, cinnamon, baking powder and dried fruit then mix well.
4. Grease a 2 lb. loaf pan with oil and spread the dough in the pan.
5. Bake the dough for 20 minutes in the oven.
6. Cover this loaf pan with aluminum foil and bake for another 20 minutes.
7. Allow the loaf to cool then slice.
8. Serve.

Nutritional Value (Amount per Serving):

Calories 387; Fat 12.1g; Cholesterol 0mg; Carbohydrate 67.3g; Sugars 27g ; Protein 5g

MINCEMEAT BANANA BREAD

Preparation Time: 15 minutes
Cooking Time: 60 minutes
Serve: 8

Ingredients:
- 5 oz. butter, softened
- 3 oz. caster sugar
- 2 large eggs, beaten
- 5 oz. self-rising flour
- 1 teaspoon baking powder
- 1 teaspoon mixed spice
- 2 ripe bananas (7 oz.), peeled and mashed
- 5 oz. mincemeat

Directions:
1. At 390 degrees F, preheat your oven.
2. Grease a 2 lb. loaf pan with oil and layer it with a parchment paper.
3. Beat butter with sugar in a mixer until fluffy.
4. Stir in egg, flour, mixed spices, baking powder, bananas and mincemeat then mix well.
5. Spread this dough in the loaf pan and bake for 1 hour.
6. Slice and serve warm.

Nutritional Value (Amount per Serving):
Calories 307; Fat 16.7g; Cholesterol 87mg; Carbohydrate 37.5g; Sugars 19.3g; Protein 4g

GLUTEN-FREE BREAD

Preparation Time: 10 minutes
Cooking Time: 60 minutes
Serve: 12

Ingredients:

- 4 small ripe bananas, mashed
- 5 oz. gluten-free self-rising flour
- 3 1/2 oz. gluten-free oats
- 1 2/3 oz. ground almonds
- 1 teaspoon gluten-free baking powder
- 1 teaspoon cinnamon
- 3 oz. dark brown sugar
- 3 oz. caster sugar
- 3 1/2 oz. butter, melted
- 2 large eggs, beaten

Topping

- 1 tablespoon icing sugar
- 1 banana, sliced

Directions:

1. At 390 degrees F, preheat your oven.
2. Grease a 2 lbs. loaf pan with oil and layer with a parchment paper.
3. Mix mashed bananas with eggs and rest of the ingredients in a bowl.
4. Spread the dough in the loaf pan and top it with banana slices and icing sugar.
5. Bake the dough for 1 hr. in the preheated oven.
6. Slice and serve.

Nutritional Value (Amount per Serving):

Calories 241; Fat 10g; Cholesterol 49mg; Carbohydrate 37.3g; Sugars 20.2g; Protein 2.9g

COCONUT CARDAMOM BREAD

Preparation Time: 10 minutes
Cooking Time: 1 hr. 10 minutes
Serve: 8

Ingredients:
- 4 1/3 oz. coconut oil
- 2 large very ripe bananas
- 3 medium eggs
- 4 1/3 oz. golden caster sugar
- 2 tablespoons coconut yogurt
- 7 oz. plain flour
- 2 teaspoons baking powder
- Seeds from 12 cardamom pods, crushed

Directions:
1. At 380 degrees F, preheat your oven.
2. Grease a 2 lbs. loaf pan with butter and layer it with parchment paper.
3. Mash 2 bananas in a mixing bowl then add eggs, yogurt, flour, baking powder, sugar and cardamom then mix well.
4. Spread this soft dough in the prepared pan and bake for 1 hr. 10 minutes in the oven.
5. Allow the dough to cool then slice and serve.

Nutritional Value (Amount per Serving):
Calories 361; Fat 18.6g; Cholesterol 61mg; Carbohydrate 45.7g; Sugars 22.4g; Protein 5.9g

STICKY TOFFEE BREAD

Preparation Time: 15 minutes
Cooking Time: 1 hr. 15 minutes
Serve: 8

Ingredients:

- 4 1/3 oz. soft butter
- 2 oz. caster sugar
- 1 2/3 oz. dark brown soft sugar
- 3 medium eggs
- 2 large ripe bananas, mashed
- 1 2/3 oz. natural yogurt
- 7 oz. plain flour
- 2 teaspoons baking powder
- 1 2/3 oz. pitted dates, chopped
- 1 2/3 oz. pecans or walnuts, chopped

Toffee sauce

- 3 1/2 oz. light brown soft sugar
- 2/3 oz. butter, cut into cubes
- 1/2 cup double cream

Banana & nut brittle

- 5 oz. caster sugar
- 1 2/3 oz. pecan, chopped
- 1 2/3 oz. banana chips
- ½ teaspoons sea salt flakes

Directions:

1. At 380 degrees F, preheat your oven.

2. Grease a 2 lbs. loaf pan with butter and layer it with parchment paper.

3. Beat butter with 2 oz. sugar in a bowl with an electric mixer for 5 minutes.

4. Stir in yogurt, banana and eggs then mix well.

5. Add baking powder, flour, nuts and dates then spread this dough in the pan.

6. Bake the dough for 1 hr. 15 minutes in the oven

7. Meanwhile, mix brown sugar and butter in a saucepan and cook until it bubbles.

8. Allow the coffee sauce to cool.

9. For the brittle, spread sugar in a frying pan and add 2 tablespoons water.

10. Cook for almost 10 minutes on a simmer then pour into a baking pan, drizzle nuts and banana chips on top then allow the sugar to cool.

11. Break the sugar brittle into pieces.

12. Drizzle the sauce over the bread and garnish with brittle.

13. Serve.

Nutritional Value (Amount per Serving):
Calories 313; Fat 6.3g; Cholesterol 57mg; Carbohydrate 63.9g; Sugars 43.7g; Protein 4.4g

WALNUT BREAD

Preparation Time: 15 minutes
Cooking Time: 60 minutes
Serve: 8

Ingredients

- 1 2/3 oz. coconut oil
- 7 oz. self-rising flour
- 2/3 oz. ground almonds
- 1 teaspoon baking powder
- 2 oz. light muscovado sugar
- 4 dates, finely chopped
- 4 very ripe bananas, mashed
- 3 tablespoons soya milk
- 2 oz. walnut pieces, toasted

Directions:

1. At 425 degrees F, preheat your oven.
2. Grease 1 lb. loaf pan with oil and layer it with a parchment paper.
3. Mix almonds with dates, sugar, baking powder and flour in a bowl.
4. Stir in oil, mashed banana and soy milk then mix well.
5. Fold in walnuts and spread this dough in the loaf pan and bake for 1 hour.
6. Allow the bread to cool then serve.

Nutritional Value (Amount per Serving):

Calories 414; Fat 18.5g; Cholesterol 0mg; Carbohydrate 58.6g; Sugars 23.9g; Protein 8.4g

ZUCCHINIS CHEDDAR BREAD

Preparation Time: 15 minutes
Cooking Time: 40 minutes
Serve: 8

Ingredients:

- 14 oz. self-rising flour
- 2 medium Zucchinis
- 1 2/3 oz. rolled oat
- 1 ½ teaspoons bicarbonate of soda
- 2 oz. mature cheddar, grated
- 1 small bunch thyme, chopped
- 1 cup pot buttermilk
- 1 tablespoon clear honey
- 1 egg, beaten

Directions:

1. At 420 degrees F, preheat your oven.
2. Dust a baking sheet with flour.
3. Grate the Zucchinis and spread the shreds on paper towels.
4. Mix flour, 1 teaspoon salt, bicarb and oats in a large bowl.
5. Stir in Zucchinis, thyme and cheddar then mix well.
6. Add honey and buttermilk then mix until lump-free.
7. Knead this dough on a floured surface then shape it into a loaf.
8. Place this loaf in the baking sheet and brush the top with egg.
9. Bake for almost 40 minutes in the preheated oven.
10. Serve.

Nutritional Value (Amount per Serving):

Calories 491; Fat 4.3g; Cholesterol 48mg ; Carbohydrate 92.8g; Sugars 6.5g; Protein 19.3g

MONKEY BREAD

Preparation Time: 15 minutes
Cooking Time: 35 minutes
Serve: 6-8

Ingredients:

Dough

- 2/3 cup semi-skimmed milk
- 1 2/3 oz. unsalted butter
- 2 large eggs
- 19 1/3 oz. strong white bread flour
- 2½ teaspoons fast-action dried yeast
- 1 2/3 oz. golden caster sugar
- Cooking oil, for greasing

To assemble

- 4 1/3 oz. unsalted butter, plus extra for greasing
- 1 tablespoon ground cinnamon
- 1 teaspoon ground ginger
- 1 teaspoon ground nutmeg
- 8 oz. light muscovado sugar
- 5 oz. pecans, toasted and chopped

Glaze

- 3 1/2 oz. icing sugar, sifted
- ½ teaspoons vanilla extract
- 1 tablespoon semi-skimmed milk
- 1 pinch cinnamon
- 2 tablespoons unsalted butter, melted

Directions:

1. Mix butter with milk in a pan and cook for 2 minutes until the butter is melted.

2. Allow this milk to cool then add eggs and all the dry ingredients.

3. Mix well to make a dough then knead for 10 minutes.

4. Place the dough in a greased bowl, cover with a plastic sheet and leave for 1 hour.

5. Grease a 25 cm Bundt pan with butter.
6. Melt remaining butter in a bowl by heating in the microwave.
7. Stir in sugar and spices then mix well.
8. Spread the butter mixture in the pan and spread 4 tablespoons pecans on top.
9. Divide the dough into 65 small pieces and roll each into balls.
10. Stack the dough balls in the Bundt pan and spread remaining nuts on top.
11. Cover the pan with a clingfilm and leave for 1 hour.
12. At 380 degrees F, preheat your oven.
13. Bake the monkey bread for 35 minutes in the oven.
14. Mix the glaze ingredients in a pan and for 2 minutes.
15. Brush this glazed over the monkey bread.
16. Serve.

Nutritional Value (Amount per Serving):
Calories 367; Fat 15.8g; Cholesterol 46mg; Carbohydrate 66g; Sugars 32.3g; Protein 8.5g

CARROT BREAD

Preparation Time: 15 minutes
Cooking Time: 65 minutes
Serve: 6

Ingredients:

- 2 cups flour
- 1 cup sugar
- 1 ½ teaspoons baking soda
- 1 ½ teaspoons cinnamon
- 1 teaspoon salt
- ½ teaspoon pumpkin pie spice
- 2 ½ cups carrots grated
- 3 eggs
- ¾ cup vegetable oil
- ¼ cup milk
- 1 teaspoon vanilla
- ¾ cup walnuts chopped

Directions:

1. At 350 degrees F, preheat your oven.
2. Layer a 9x5 inches loaf pan with parchment paper.
3. Beat eggs with vanilla, milk and oil in a large bowl.
4. Stir in dry ingredients then mix until smooth.
5. Fold in walnuts and carrots then transfer this batter to the loaf pan.
6. Bake the carrot bread for 65 minutes in the preheated oven.
7. Allow the cake to cool then slice and serve.

Nutritional Value (Amount per Serving):

Calories 256; Fat 0.6g; Cholesterol 0mg; Carbohydrate 34.5g; Sugars 3.6g; Protein 5.2g

SAVORY PIES, TARTS, AND PIZZA

HOLIDAY PIZZAS

Preparation Time: 10 minutes
Cooking Time: 15 minutes
Serve: 8

Ingredients:

Dough

- 1 lb. strong white bread flour
- 1 small pinch of sugar
- 1 sachet fast-action dried yeast
- 2 tablespoons olive oil
- 1 1/4 cup warm water

Sauce

- 1 garlic clove, minced
- 1 2/3 cup chunky passata
- 1 tablespoon tomato purée
- 1 teaspoon dried oregano
- handful basil leaves , snipped
- 1 small pinch of sugar
- 1 teaspoon red wine vinegar

Toppings

- 1/2 cup ham, diced
- ½ cup red peppers, chopped
- 2 tablespoons black olives, sliced
- ½ cup mozzarella , shredded
- 4 cherry tomatoes, sliced
- ½ cup cheddar, shredded tuna

Directions:

1. For dough, mix water, yeast and sugar in a bowl and leave for 5 minutes.

2. Stir in flour and olive oil then mix until it makes a sticky dough.

3. Knead this dough on a lightly flour surface then transfer to a greased bowl.
4. Cover this bowl with a plastic sheet then leave this dough for 1 hour.
5. Mix all the tomato sauce ingredients in a bowl.
6. At 420 degrees F, preheat your oven.
7. Divide this dough into two portions and Spread them into 2 greased pizza pans.
8. Spread the tomato sauce on top of the pizza doughs and
9. Add ham and other toppings on top of the sauce.
10. Bake the pizzas for 15 minutes until the pizza edges turn golden brown.
11. Serve.

Nutritional Value (Amount per Serving):
Calories 234; Fat 7.7g; Cholesterol 0mg; Carbohydrate 36g; Sugars 1.8g; Protein 6.1g

QUICK PITTA PIZZAS

Preparation Time: 15 minutes
Cooking Time: 10 minutes
Serve: 4

Ingredients:

- 4 wholewheat pitta breads
- 4 teaspoons sun-dried tomato purée
- 3 ripe plum tomatoes, diced
- 1 shallot, sliced
- 1 2/3 oz. chorizo, diced
- 1 2/3 oz. mature cheddar, grated
- few basil leaves, to garnish

Directions:

1. At 430 degrees F, preheat your oven.
2. Grease a baking sheet with cooking oil.
3. Place the pitta breads on the baking sheet.
4. Spread 1 teaspoon tomato puree on top of each pita bread.
5. Divide tomatoes, cheddar, chorizo and shallot on top of the bread.
6. Bake the pizza's for 10 minutes in the oven.
7. Garnish with basil and serve.

Nutritional Value (Amount per Serving):

Calories 267; Fat 9.9g; Cholesterol 22mg ; Carbohydrate 29.9g; Sugars 3.8g; Protein 14.2g

RAINBOW PIZZAS

Preparation Time: 15 minutes
Cooking Time: 20 minutes
Serve: 4

Ingredients:
- 2 plain pizza bases
- 6 tablespoons passata
- 14 oz. mixed red and yellow tomatoes, sliced
- 2 oz. sprouting broccoli, stems sliced
- 8 green olives, pitted and halved
- 5 oz. mozzarella cherries
- 2 tablespoons fresh pesto
- 1 handful fresh basil leaves, to serve

Directions:
1. At 370 degrees F, preheat your oven.
2. Spread the pizza crust in a greased baking sheet.
3. Spread half of the passata on top each pizza crust.
4. Divide the tomato slices, broccoli, olives, mozzarella, pesto and basil on top of the crust.
5. Bake the pizzas for 20 minutes in the preheated oven.
6. Serve warm.

Nutritional Value (Amount per Serving):
Calories 352; Fat 15.3g; Cholesterol 28mg; Carbohydrate 42.8g; Sugars 3.3g; Protein 11.5g

TUNA ROCKET PIZZAS

Preparation Time: 15 minutes
Cooking Time: 12 minutes
Serve: 6

Ingredients:
- 2 readymade pizza dough crusts
- 2 tablespoons tomato purée
- 4 oz. can tuna in oil, drained, oil reserved
- Plain flour , for dusting
- 1 tablespoon caper
- 4 1/3 oz. pack value mozzarella
- 10 pitted black kalamata olives
- 1 red onion , thinly sliced
- 1 small handful rocket

Directions:
1. At 450 degrees F, preheat your oven.
2. Spread each pizza dough crust in a greased baking sheet.
3. Mix tomato puree with 4 tablespoons water, and 1 tablespoon tuna oil in a bowl.
4. Spread half of the tomato puree, tuna, capers, cheese and olives on top.
5. Bake the pizzas for 12 minutes in the oven.
6. Garnish with rockets and onion.
7. Slice and serve warm.

Nutritional Value (Amount per Serving):
Calories 303; Fat 47.3g; Cholesterol 34mg; Carbohydrate 20.1g   ; Sugars 3.6g; Protein 22.6g

MOZZARELLA, HAM PESTO PIZZAS

Preparation Time: 15 minutes
Cooking Time: 5 minutes
Serve: 4

Ingredients:
- 4 mini pitta breads
- 5 oz. pack mozzarella
- 4 teaspoons pesto
- 2 oz. smoked wafer thin ham

Directions:
1. At 350 degrees F, preheat your oven.
2. Add 1 teaspoon pesto, a mozzarella slice, and ham on top.
3. Drizzle black pepper on top and place the pita bread pizzas in the grill again.
4. Place the pitta pizza in a greased baking sheet and bake for 5 minutes.
5. Serve warm.

Nutritional Value (Amount per Serving):
Calories 384; Fat 19.4g; Cholesterol 79mg; Carbohydrate 25.7g; Sugars 2.2g; Protein 24.8g

BACON SCONE PIZZA

Preparation Time: 15 minutes
Cooking Time: 20 minutes
Serve: 6

Ingredients:

Scone base

- 9 oz. plain flour
- 1 teaspoon salt
- 2 teaspoons baking powder
- 1 2/3 oz. butter, chopped
- 2 eggs
- 3 tablespoons milk

Cheesy topping

- 1 tablespoon olive oil
- 1 green pepper, quartered, sliced
- 4 rashers streaky bacon, chopped
- 5 spring onions, sliced
- 2 tablespoons tomato ketchup
- 2 tablespoons tomato purée
- 8 cherry tomatoes, halved
- 2 oz. mature cheddar, grated

Directions:

1. At 430 degrees F, preheat your oven.
2. Mix flour with 1 tsp salt and baking powder in a bowl.
3. Stir in butter then mix well.
4. Fold in eggs and milk then mix until they make a smooth dough.
5. Knead this dough on a floured surface and spread this dough in a greased baking sheet.
6. Sauté bacon with pepper and oil in a frying pan for 5 minutes.
7. Stir in spring onion and mix well.
8. Spread the ketchup on the pizza base and add the bacon mixture.

9. Add tomatoes and cheese on top then bake for 15 minutes.
10. Serve warm.

Nutritional Value (Amount per Serving):
Calories 317; Fat 15.1g; Cholesterol 78mg; Carbohydrate 29.9g; Sugars 4.4g; Protein 15.4g

SPINACH PIZZA

Preparation Time: 15 minutes
Cooking Time: 15 minutes
Serve: 8

Ingredients:
- 14 oz. spinach
- 1 sachet fast-action dried yeast
- 1 lb. strong white bread flour

Spinach pesto
- 1 large bunch of basil
- 1 2/3 oz. pine nuts, toasted
- 1 2/3 oz. parmesan, grated
- 1/2 cup olive oil
- 1 lemon, zested and juiced
- 2 garlic cloves, chopped

Toppings
- 7 oz. crème fraiche
- 10 1/2 oz. long-stemmed broccoli, halved if thick
- 7 oz. cherry tomatoes, halved
- 7 oz. ball mozzarella, torn
- ½ teaspoons chilli flakes
- Olive oil, for drizzling

Directions:
1. Add spinach to a pot filled with boiling water then remove after 30 seconds.
2. Blend spinach with 2/3 cup hot water in a blender until smooth.
3. Mix yeast with 2 tablespoons tepid water in a mixing bowl.
4. Stir in spinach puree, 2 teaspoons salt, flour and 1/4 cup water then mix well until it makes a smooth dough.
5. Knead this dough for 5 minutes then transfer to a greased bowl.
6. Cover this bowl with a plastic sheet and leave for 1 hour.
7. Blend the pesto ingredients in a blender until smooth.

8. Punch down the dough and divide the into two portions.
9. Spread each portion into a greased baking sheet.
10. At 350 degrees F, preheat your oven.
11. Spread the pesto over the dough bases.
12. Divide the toppings on top of the pesto then bake for 15 minutes.
13. Serve warm.

Nutritional Value (Amount per Serving):
Calories 409; Fat 18.8g; Cholesterol 4mg ; Carbohydrate 50.1g; Sugars 1.5g; Protein 12.2g

SPINACH BLUE CHEESE PIZZA

Preparation Time: 15 minutes
Cooking Time: 19 minutes
Serve: 8

Ingredients:
- 1 teaspoon rapeseed oil
- 2 large flat mushrooms, halved and sliced
- 2 garlic cloves , chopped
- 6 oz. spinach,
- 1 red onion, halved and sliced
- ½ oz. vegetarian blue cheese , crumbled
- 4 walnut halves , broken

Base
- 4 1/3 oz. wholewheat spelt flour
- ½ teaspoons baking powder
- 3 tablespoons bio yogurt
- 3 tablespoons water

Directions:
1. At 430 degrees F, preheat your oven.
2. Grease a baking sheet with cooking oil.
3. Sauté garlic and mushrooms with oil in a skillet for 5 minutes.
4. Stir in spinach and onion then cook for 2 minutes.
5. Mix spelt flour, baking powder, yogurt and water in a bowl until smooth.
6. Spread dough in the baking sheet into a ¼ inch thick sheet.
7. Spread the spinach mixture, cheese and walnut on top.
8. Bake this pizza for 12 minutes in the preheated oven.
9. Serve warm.

Nutritional Value (Amount per Serving):
Calories 236; Fat 9.6g; Cholesterol 8mg; Carbohydrate 29g; Sugars 2.4g; Protein 11.3g

CAULIFLOWER CHEESE PIZZA

Preparation Time: 10 minutes
Cooking Time: 65 minutes
Serve: 6

Ingredients:
- 1 tablespoon oil
- 1 garlic clove, crushed
- 1 large cauliflower, trimmed and chopped
- 4 tablespoons mascarpone
- 2 small pizza bases
- 1 2/3 oz. vegetarian hard cheese

Directions:
1. At 430 degrees F, preheat your oven.
2. Mix garlic with cauliflower, and oil in a baking sheet then bake for 45 minutes.
3. Spread the pizza base in another greased baking pan.
4. Add mascarpone, cauliflower and hard cheese on top.
5. Bake the pizza for 20 minutes in the preheated oven.
6. Slice and serve warm.

Nutritional Value (Amount per Serving):
Calories 373; Fat 18.9g; Cholesterol 16mg; Carbohydrate 37.3g; Sugars 3.3g; Protein 15.4g

FIORENTINA PIZZAS

Preparation Time: 10 minutes
Cooking Time: 10 minutes
Serve: 2

Ingredients:
- 9 oz. bag spinach
- 2 large Middle Eastern flatbreads
- 1 pinch nutmeg
- 2 eggs
- 1 2/3 oz. Gruyère, grated
- 4 prosciutto slices, torn

Directions:
1. At 430 degrees F, preheat your oven.
2. Spread the flatbreads in a baking sheet.
3. Add spinach, nutmeg, and salt on top of the bread.
4. Crack an egg at the center of each bread.
5. Drizzle the cheese and black pepper on top.
6. Bake for 10 minutes in the preheated oven and garnish with prosciutto.
7. Serve warm.

Nutritional Value (Amount per Serving):
Calories 242; Fat 7.9g; Cholesterol 164mg; Carbohydrate 32g; Sugars 1.9g; Protein 13.1g

EASY DINNERS

SAUSAGE PASTA DINNER

Preparation Time: 10 minutes
Cooking Time: 20 minutes
Serve: 8

Ingredients:
- 1 tablespoon olive oil
- 3 tablespoons onion, chopped
- 1 package polish sausage, sliced
- 2 cloves garlic, minced
- 1 (14 oz) can fire roasted tomatoes
- 8 oz. pasta
- 2 cup water
- 2 teaspoons chicken bouillon powder
- 1/2 cup milk
- 1 1/2 cup cheddar cheese, grated

Directions:
1. Boil 8 oz. pasta with 2 cups water in a saucepan for 10 minutes then drain.
2. Spread pasta in the casserole dish then top it with onion, garlic, tomatoes, olive oil, and sausage.
3. Mix milk with chicken bouillon powder and pour over the pasta.
4. Drizzle cheese on top.
5. Bake the pasta casserole for 10 minutes in the oven.
6. Serve warm.

Nutritional Value (Amount per Serving):
Calories 448; Fat 23g; Cholesterol 91mg; Carbohydrate 41.3g; Sugars 5.4g; Protein 20.5g

BAKED CHICKEN PARMESAN

Preparation Time: 15 minutes
Cooking Time: 12 minutes
Serve: 8

Ingredients:
- 2 lbs. boneless chicken cutlets
- 2 eggs
- 1/4 cup milk
- 1 1/4 cup Italian seasoned breadcrumbs
- 1 1/4 teaspoons garlic powder
- 2 oz. shaved Parmesan
- 12 oz. marinara sauce
- 6 oz. mozzarella cheese, shredded

Directions:
1. At 400 degrees F, preheat your oven.
2. Grease a baking sheet with cooking oil.
3. Beat eggs with milk in a suitable bowl.
4. Mix breadcrumbs with garlic powder in a bowl.
5. Dip the chicken first in the prepared egg mixture then coat with the breadcrumbs.
6. Place the breaded chicken in a greased baking sheet then bake for 10 minutes.
7. Now drizzle marinara sauce and mozzarella cheese on top.
8. Bake the chicken for 12 minutes in the preheated oven.
9. Garnish with parsley, and basil then serve.

Nutritional Value (Amount per Serving):
Calories 371; Fat 13.4g; Cholesterol 125mg; Carbohydrate 27g; Sugars 7.2g; Protein 35.9g

CHICKEN RICE CASSEROLE

Preparation Time: 15 minutes
Cooking Time: 1 hr. 30 minutes
Serve: 8

Ingredients:

- 1 1/2 cups long grain white rice
- 2 cans cream of chicken soup
- 1 cup water
- 2 cups milk
- 1 packet onion soup mix
- 1 1/2 cups shredded cheddar cheese
- 3 thick boneless chicken breasts
- Salt and black pepper, to taste

Directions:

1. At 350 degrees F, preheat your oven.
2. Grease a 9x13 inches baking pan with cooking spray.
3. Mix onion soup, water, milk, cream of soups and rice in a bowl.
4. Spread this mixture in the prepared pan and drizzle cheese on top.
5. Place the chicken breasts in this rice mixture.
6. Cover this chicken dish with the aluminum foil and bake for 1 hr. 30 minutes.
7. Uncover and drizzle remaining cheese on top.
8. Serve warm.

Nutritional Value (Amount per Serving):

Calories 393; Fat 14.5g; Cholesterol 74mg; Carbohydrate 37.1g; Sugars 3.4g; Protein 26.8g

CRISPY CHICKEN TENDERS

Preparation Time: 15 minutes
Cooking Time: 18 minutes
Serve: 4

Ingredients:
- ½ cup all-purpose flour
- 3 large eggs
- 3 tablespoons water
- 2 teaspoons paprika
- 1 ½ teaspoons garlic powder
- ½ teaspoon onion powder
- 1 teaspoon salt
- ¼ teaspoon black pepper
- 2 cups panko bread crumbs
- 2 pounds chicken tenders

Directions:
1. At 425 degrees F, preheat your oven.
2. Set a suitable wire rack in a rimmed baking sheet and grease it with cooking spray.
3. Spread flour in a shallow bowl, beat eggs with black pepper, salt, onion powder, garlic powder and paprika in a bowl.
4. Spread the breadcrumbs in a plate.
5. Coat the chicken with flour first then dip in the egg mixture and finally coat with the breadcrumbs.
6. Place the coated chicken on this set wire rack and bake for 18 minutes in the oven.
7. Serve warm.

Nutritional Value (Amount per Serving):
Calories 465; Fat 12.1g; Cholesterol 202mg; Carbohydrate 52.8g; Sugars 4.2g; Protein 34.2g

CREAMY PASTA BAKE

Preparation Time: 15 minutes
Cooking Time: 35 minutes
Serve: 6

Ingredients:

- 2 cups leftover shredded chicken
- 9 oz. dried macaroni pasta
- 1 pinch of fine salt
- 4 rashers smoked bacon, chopped
- 2 large garlic cloves crushed
- 1 teaspoon fresh rosemary, chopped
- 1 1/4 cups pure cream
- 2 teaspoons butter
- ⅔ cup fresh parmesan cheese grated
- ⅓ cup mozzarella, shredded

Directions:

1. At 355 degrees F, preheat your oven.
2. Boil the pasta as per the package's instruction until the pasta turns soft then drain.
3. Meanwhile, sauté bacon in a skillet for 8 minutes.
4. Stir in rosemary and garlic then cook for 1 minute.
5. Add the cooked pasta to the bacon along with cream, chicken and parmesan.
6. Mix well and spread this mixture in a baking dish.
7. Drizzle mozzarella cheese on top and bake for 20 minutes in the oven.
8. Serve warm.

Nutritional Value (Amount per Serving):

Calories 352; Fat 11.9g; Cholesterol 62mg; Carbohydrate 35.6g; Sugars 0.4g; Protein 24.6g

ROASTED SALMON

Preparation Time: 15 minutes
Cooking Time: 12 minutes
Serve: 4

Ingredients:
- 4 tablespoons unsalted butter
- Coarse salt and ground pepper, to taste
- 1 (3 pounds) salmon fillet, skin on
- Chopped fresh parsley leaves, for serving

Directions:
1. At 375 degrees F, preheat your oven.

2. Grease a rimmed baking sheet with butter.

3. Place the salmon in the baking sheet and brush the fish with butter, black pepper and salt.

4. Bake the salmon for 12 minutes in the preheated oven.

5. Garnish with parsley and serve warm.

Nutritional Value (Amount per Serving):
Calories 337; Fat 22.5g; Cholesterol 109mg; Carbohydrate 0g; Sugars 0g; Protein 34.7g

CHICKEN NUGGETS

Preparation Time: 15 minutes
Cooking Time: 20 minutes
Serve: 8

Ingredients:

- 2 boneless chicken breasts
- 1 cup panko Japanese breadcrumbs
- 1/3 cup grated Parmesan
- Coarse salt, to taste
- 1 tablespoon vegetable oil
- 1/2 cup all-purpose flour
- 3 large eggs, beaten
- Cooking spray
- Honey Mustard, for serving

Directions:

1. At 400 degrees F, preheat your oven.
2. Spread the panko in a rimmed baking sheet and bake for 8 minutes.
3. Transfer the crumbs to a shallow dish then add ½ teaspoons salt, parmesan and oil.
4. Spread flour in another plate and beat eggs in a shallow dish.
5. Coat the prepared chicken with flour, dip in the egg and then coat with the breadcrumbs.
6. Place the coated thicken in the rimmed baking sheet.
7. Bake the chicken for 12 minutes in the oven.
8. Serve warm.

Nutritional Value (Amount per Serving):

Calories 315; Fat 14.2g; Cholesterol 207mg; Carbohydrate 16.2g; Sugars 0.5g; Protein 29.3g

BARBECUED CHICKEN

Preparation Time: 15 minutes
Cooking Time: 20 minutes
Serve: 4

Ingredients:
- 2 teaspoon onion powder
- 2 teaspoons garlic powder
- 2/3 cup molasses
- 1 1/2 cup ketchup
- 1/3 cup brown sugar
- 3 tablespoons honey mustard
- 1/3 cup cider vinegar
- 2 teaspoons ground black pepper
- 2 lbs. boneless chicken breast, diced

Directions:
1. At 350 degrees F, preheat your oven.
2. Mix molasses, ketchup, honey, vinegar, black pepper, garlic powder and onion powder in a bowl.
3. Place the cleaned chicken in the marinade and mix well to coat.
4. Set a grill rack in a baking sheet and place the chicken on the rack.
5. Bake the chicken for almost 20 minutes in the oven.
6. Serve warm.

Nutritional Value (Amount per Serving):
Calories 314; Fat 3.7g; Cholesterol 42mg; Carbohydrate 56.3g; Sugars 44.3g; Protein 15g

PARSLEY COD

Preparation Time: 10 minutes
Cooking Time: 15 minutes
Serve: 4

Ingredients:
- 3 tablespoons lemon juice
- 3 tablespoons butter, melted
- 1/4 cup all-purpose flour
- 1/2 teaspoon salt
- 1/4 teaspoon paprika
- 1/4 teaspoon lemon-pepper seasoning
- 4 (6 ounces) cod fillets
- 2 tablespoons minced fresh parsley
- 2 teaspoons grated lemon zest

Directions:
1. At 400 degrees F, preheat your oven.
2. Mix lemon juice and butter in a shallow bowl.
3. Whisk flour with seasonings in another bowl.
4. Coat the fish with lemon juice mixture and coat with the flour mixture.
5. Place the coated fish in a casserole dish then pour the remaining lemon juice mixture on top.
6. Bake the fish for almost 15 minutes in the preheated oven.
7. Serve warm.

Nutritional Value (Amount per Serving):
Calories 200; Fat 9.9g; Cholesterol 78mg; Carbohydrate 6.7g; Sugars 0.4g; Protein 21.1g

MEAT LOAF MUFFINS

Preparation Time: 10 minutes
Cooking Time: 22 minutes
Serve: 6

Ingredients:

- 1 large egg, beaten
- 1/2 cup dry bread crumbs
- 1/2 cup finely chopped onion
- 1/2 cup finely chopped green pepper
- 1/4 cup barbecue sauce
- 1-1/2 pounds lean ground beef
- 3 tablespoons ketchup

Directions:

1. At 375 degrees F, preheat your oven.
2. Mix beef with barbecue sauce, green pepper, onion, egg and breadcrumbs in a bowl.
3. Divide this beef mixture in a 12 cup muffin tray.
4. Bake the meatloaves for 15 minutes then brush the meatloaves with ketchup.
5. Continue baking them for 7 minutes in the oven.
6. Serve warm.

Nutritional Value (Amount per Serving):

Calories 216; Fat 6.1g; Cholesterol 99mg; Carbohydrate 13.5g; Sugars 5.6g; Protein 25.5g

CONCLUSION

Are you ready to enjoy some sweet and savoury homemade treats? Well, now you can make it all by yourself using all the above given easy to bake recipes. Now all you need to do is to set up your oven, adjust its heat and ready the food to get it baked! Don't forget to put on those oven mittens and enjoy the best of the pies, cakes, cookies, breakfast treats and dinners meal.

Made in the USA
Monee, IL
17 September 2022

c6dc2433-ff6f-466e-8d2c-854145f05aaeR02